I want to dedicate this book to you, the person reading this.

You matter.

You always have.

And you always will.

CONTENTS

INTRODUCTION

They say when you point your finger at somebody, you have three fingers pointing back at you. Throughout this life, these are the things I've learned:

- The best way to help a person is to **love them**.
- Just listening in order to speak isn't always the way to go. Sometimes you have to "listen to understand," otherwise you may start to "listen and judge."
- Instead of throwing stones, we should try burying them. Stones were never meant for us to throw.
- Sometimes the stones we throw at other people are the stones that are really meant to harm us.
- It's easy to see another person's mistakes, but it's harder to see our own faults.
- Sharing your scars will free others. Showing their scars will bring conflict.

This poetry book is centered on thoughts, experiences, and reflection. Some stories you may relate to, while other stories you may not. However you read it, this poetry book gives us a chance to reflect upon our own lives.

NO LONGER WOUNDED

I'm so nice to look at like palm trees
That sounded so conceited
But I can give you reason after reason
Cause after God created me I know now who I came to be
And I will never ever look the same to me
People come complain to me thinking I'll sit and agree
But that's something that's no longer in my pedigree
Couple folks could've made it out if they just bled with me
But they was too scarred
Some could never give that life up and they was too gone
Now they paying for their mistakes and ain't got no Groupons
As for me, I'm moving forward with or without shoes on
Watch my life, catch the flight as I see the sun set
On my way to paradise though I ain't seen the Son yet
I just know they say that one day He gon' come back
And I can't wait to see the world and just how He runs that
If it ain't in my life, that means I don't need that
If they hate what I'm about, then forget the feedback
I'ma live a life of faith, it may be hard to see that
But I'ma show the world God is real and you best believe that

NOTE TO SELF

How we see ourselves is very important in this life. Some will believe in us. Others will tear us down. But what we say to ourselves every day is what separates the achiever from the dreamer.

WORKSHOP

1. How do you see yourself?

_____

_____

_____

_____

_____

2. What would your life look like if you reached your full potential?

_____

_____

_____

_____

_____

3. What's stopping you from reaching your full potential?

_____

_____

_____

_____

_____

FOR THREE DAYS, LISTEN TO THE THINGS THAT YOU THINK AND SAY ABOUT YOURSELF. WHEN PEOPLE SAY THINGS ABOUT YOU, DOES YOUR VIEWPOINT ABOUT YOURSELF CHANGE? THE FIRST STEP TO REACHING YOUR FULL POTENTIAL IS CHANGING HOW YOU THINK ABOUT AND SPEAK TO YOURSELF.

HOW BAD DO YOU WANT IT?

Look at you all

Young men and women just sitting there listening

Hoping that I say the right words to grab your attention

And spark something on the inside of you that's always been there from the
beginning

Dreams, hidden potential, who knows?

My question to you is: *What are you waiting for?*

Cause last time I checked you don't need to have a résumé filled out in order to
chase the impossible

So tell me what's stopping you?

Has it ever occurred to you that maybe it's not so much you waiting on God, but it's
God waiting on you?

I mean, he says in his heart a man plans his course and the Lord orders his steps,
but . . .

How is it that you've been waiting on God this entire time when you never told him
what it is that you wanna do in life?

I mean, that don't sound right if you ask me

I mean, I know there's a lot of people out there that got a dream but all they wanna
do is talk about it, they don't wanna be about it

And I'm tired of hearing people talk about it cause nobody wants to take action in
order to make it happen

So how bad do you really want it?

If your dream was right there in front of you, would you take the steps to reach it?

Or would you just envision yourself daydreaming like you're in it?

When every tool that you need is right there in front of you but you don't use it
cause you think everything is supposed to be given to you

And you sit there and act like nothing in your life happens and wonder why failure's
on your mind, but it only comes cause you don't practice

Cause you don't put in the work!

So how bad do you really want it?

If you had to sacrifice almost everything, you had to go on a fast and get closer to
God, would you do it?

You say yes, but when your mind tells you to go on a fast, you begin to second-
guess yourself and act clueless

Like you don't know what you're talking about

Think about it

If opportunity knocked, would you answer before you said "Who is it?"

Or would you look through the window and the peephole, open the door,
opportunity's gone, and you missed it?

Which one are you?

Cause all I'm seeing is people start stuff, but they don't ever finish it

Talking about being successful, but they don't even live it

So how bad do you really want it?

Do you believe in yourself, or are you still looking for help?

And why is it that when you fail, you blame others for your mistakes when the only
person who can stop you from who you want to be in life is yourself?

How bad do you really want it?

If you were the only one who believed that you could live out your dream, would
you still chase it?

Or are you one of those people who hangs out with those who shoot down your
dreams and you just sit there and take it?

And you give up and say you're not going to make it

How bad do you really want it?

If the person right next to you had your success in his hands and could get you to
where you wanted to be in life, would you ask 'em?

Or would you just stand there, close your mouth, wave at 'em, and let them walk
past you?

You say that you would ask 'em, but God has your success right in his hand,

And he's telling you that you're a winner when you keep saying that you're a loser, failing, trying to do it by yourself,

Not relying on God when he says I got plans to give you a hope and a future

How bad do you really want it?

If God told you to walk by faith for a couple of weeks, would you trust him?

Or would you lean into your own understanding and trust your own judgment?

How bad do you really want it?

Cause if you ask me, it seems like you don't want it that bad at all

And it's crazy, cause if a doctor said you only had a couple of weeks to live, you'd be out there in the world tryna do it all

Every dream that ever came to your mind

So how bad do you really want it?

Cause if you really wanted it that bad, you wouldn't let nothing stop you

And you should know that with men it's impossible, but with God all things are possible

So how bad do you really want it?

Cause the enemy will try and stop us from being who we're supposed to be, but all we gotta do is put in the work, cause God's already given us the victory

It only comes down to one thing and that's

How bad do you really want it?

So ask yourself: *How bad do you really want it?*

NOTE TO SELF

It's one thing to dream. It's another thing to talk about it. If you really want it like you say you want it, GO GET IT. HOW BAD DO YOU WANT IT?

WORKSHOP

1. How bad do you really want it?

_____

_____

_____

_____

2. Are you putting actions behind the dreams you speak?

_____

_____

_____

_____

3. Are you depending on other people?

_____

_____

_____

4. Are you networking and building connections?

_____

_____

_____

_____

ONE OF THE BEST THINGS IN LIFE
IS FINDING PURPOSE. TAKE THE
NEXT THREE DAYS TO WRITE DOWN
ALL YOUR GIFTS AND TALENTS.
ONCE YOU REALIZE WHAT YOU'RE
GOOD AT, SPEND MORE TIME
PERFECTING THOSE GIFTS
AND TALENTS.

SHOOT YOUR SHOT

Figaro Figaro

She threw the ball in my court so I decided to lay it up like I was doing a finger roll

And I know it sounds kinda crazy, but Shawty got a nice game

You see her heart is so amazing

Cause the way she play defense

It got me straddling the fence

And I'm realizing she the one I want to spend my life with

But baby girl, I need a chance

Can you give me a chance?

I'll D you up in man, but I'd rather have the ball up in my hand so I can take you to
the hole

Post you up in the lane

Show you my little jumper so you can see I got game

And you can call a timeout, but ain't nothing gon' change

And I ain't worried about the crowd and how they try to put dirt up on my name

Just cause I'm playin' away

Cause right now me and you ain't on the same team

But we both know that I'm really the one that you need

Cause you been looking for somebody who can be clutch for you

When it come down to it and I'm the one who can hit that three

So baby, if you let me, I can be your MVP

Even though right now I'm a R double-O K-I-E

But one day I hope that you see

That when it come down to you if people gon' get in the way

When I'm on a fast break I should hit 'em with a Euro step until there's no one left

But I'd rather just shoot my shot and watch it go in the net

And if I miss my shot

I'm driving to the hole next and if they end up fouling me,

I hope I fall and watch it go in the net

So I can say "and one"

And one

Yeah, I landed on a bad one

A bad one

And I know they feelin' mad, huh

They mad, huh?

Cause I finally made that basket

That basket

Now she talkin' 'bout *lay it up on me*

Just push it up on me

I see you tryna get it in

Get it in

And now you shooting for the win

Baby girl, you saw me go to the hole and I ended it with that finger roll

And they ended up fouling me so now I'm sitting at the free throw line

And my heart pounding inside

But I been training for this moment my whole life and you can see it in my eyes

And the crowd tryna distract me but I ain't tryna pay attention

I take a deep breath

Take my four dribbles and spin it

And the shot goes in

And all of a sudden we winnin' so I'm back at half court cause I'm ready to
    start defendin'

Cause girl, I ain't tryna let nobody get at you

I figured you could see it in my demeanor even though I'm tryna play it cool

And as he dribbles past half court, there's only a couple seconds left on the clock

And I'm running through all these picks tryna beat him to his favorite spot

And he tries to cross me over

But I lower my base

He takes two dribbles to the right and I cut him off right away

And he decides to spin and then he shoots a fadeaway

And I'm just watching the ball as it approaches the rim

And I'm just hoping that the shot that he took doesn't go in

And then it hits the rim

Then it starts to roll around

Then the shot ended up going in

And all I could do was just really put my head down

Cause he ended up with the girl

And I ended up with the loss

Until the ref said that the bucket didn't count

Cause he shot the ball after the buzzer went off

And I said hell yeah

Hell yeah

Hell yeah

NOTE TO SELF

Not everybody gets the chance to have the ball thrown in their court, whether it's from the girl you want or business opportunities. What I want you to know is that if you don't shoot your shot, someone else will. So the question is, are you OK with losing out on that girl or even that business opportunity based on not even trying? Or are you willing to shoot your shot and see what happens? Whether you succeed or fail, at least you took the shot. It's four seconds left to go . . . What you gon' do?

WORKSHOP

1. What have you been hesitant about?

_____

_____

_____

_____

2. What's been holding you back from shooting your shot?

_____

_____

_____

_____

3. What's the worst thing that could happen?

_____

_____

_____

_____

4. What if you make your shot?

_____

_____

_____

_____

YOU NEVER KNOW WHAT COULD HAPPEN UNTIL YOU SHOOT YOUR SHOT. YOU COULD END UP GETTING THE BOY OR GIRL OF YOUR DREAMS OR EVEN THAT BUSINESS OPPORTUNITY YOU'VE BEEN WAITING FOR. INSTEAD OF THINKING ABOUT WHAT HAPPENS IF YOU MISS THE SHOT, THINK ABOUT WHAT HAPPENS WHEN YOU MAKE THE SHOT.

LIKE FATHER, LIKE SON

She was looking for a friend

But she found a lover

Who couldn't see her for who she was until they was under covers

So they kept it secret

Like they was undercover

And nobody knew until they married each other

Then days go by

Years go by

Feelings start to change and the kid starts to cry

He said Mama, please stay

Daddy, don't you go

It'll never be the same again without both of y'all in the home

But Daddy grabs his keys

Son, Daddy gotta leave

And as you start to get older, just don't blame this on me

Cause once you grow up, one day you gon' see

That two parents can't stay together to raise a family if they ain't happy

And that's what happened with Mommy and Daddy

And even though I want to stay and watch my kid grow up

I know that if I do, then things will end badly

But Son, pay attention

Hey!!! I need you to listen

Just cause we in two different households don't mean that you can't come and visit

He said you don't understand

Daddy, we had plans

With you gone, who gon' teach me how to be a man?

You can't leave and put everything in my mama's hands

She got too much on her plate

Plus, we ain't at that place in life where we can overcome mistakes

So who gon' run the house?

Who gon' make the decisions?

Sports is my only way if you walk out that door, Pops

And if you do, then I'ma be another statistic

The door shuts . . .

The boy's crying . . .

We gon' make it, baby . . .

Mama's trying

Just stay patient

Wait in line

And when your chance come, like a star you gon' shine

That boy grew up and went to college

Got himself a degree

He was good enough in sports

So he made it to the league

He gave money to his pops

But made sure he took care of his mama

While dodging them females that wanted him for his commas that was on his
    contract

The women threw themselves at him daily, but he wasn't with all that

See, he wanted something simple

Wanted somebody basic

Who he could have fun with at home

And not only when he took her places

So he decided to take a trip

Suddenly his heart races

Cause he felt this feeling he ain't felt before

He found a woman who seemed like she had been down before

Like a ride-or-die type

Y'all know what that's like

A woman that's been walking like she was already wifed

And so he took her on a date

Come to find out she loved it

And ever since that first date, they both been feeling something

But they never made it public

They just kept it a secret

Couple months later she got pregnant and told him that she would keep it

So before it got scary, they decided to get married

But that's when stuff got real

Cause after they had the baby stuff went downhill

They started fussing

Started fighting while the baby been crying

And now the daddy feels like he just been wasting his time

His eyes filled with rage

Ever since we got married, things ain't never been the same

And I think it's best if we move on and we just go our separate ways

Cause I'm tired of always having to be the one to take the blame

She said you'll never understand

You're not a woman, you're a man

You can't just up and leave whenever things get hard, we married, man

Plus, if you go, who's gon' teach our son how to be a man?

You can't leave and put everything all in my hands

He said leave our son out of this

This between me and you

I'ma be there for our child, but I ain't gon' raise him with you

She left and went to the room

But she was crying badly

Before she closed the door, she turned around and told him, you just lost our family

He spoke those words too soon

But he only said it cause he wasn't happy
And now the little boy gotta grow up without living with his daddy
So he goes in his son's room
Instantly he cries
Picks his son up
And then he looks him in the eyes
One day you gon' get older
And you gon' ask Mommy why
And whatever she tells you, I want you to know, I'm not that type of guy
I love you with all my heart
But leaving you behind was never a part of the plan
I can only hope and pray that when you grow up
You can finally understand

The door shuts . . .
The boy's crying . . .
We gon' make it, baby . . .
Mama's trying . . .
Daddy left . . .
Yeah, Daddy's gone . . .
Pulled the same move like his pops . . .
Like father, like son

NOTE TO SELF

Not everything is your fault. Sometimes we just get put in bad situations. Whether it's a one-parent household or no-parent household, we all are given a chance to change that once we start a family. We can break the cycle, but first it starts with you.

WORTH IT

The worst feeling in the world is feeling dead but still living

The worst horror story ever told is the truth

The greatest love that we know is Jesus laying down his life

The only failure I accept is falling short

Can someone tell me what's worth fighting for?

Who's worth crying for?

And what type of love do you need to see who's worth dying for?

Is there any gas you can get to fuel faith?

Is there any weapon in this world to kill hate?

I just want to bury it

I'm tired of all this arrogance

All the things that held me down, I'm tired of tryna carry it

I just wanna feel free

I'm tired of being filthy

And giving leverage to the things in life that's tryna kill me

I'm tryna stay alive in a world that wants me dead

Right behind a system that won't let me get ahead

And now I'm feeling broke in a world that got bread

Though they take me for a joke I know I'm not a funny man

Listen loud and clear

I got people behind me like my rear

And they always side with me like my ears

And they never doubted me, success is near

We just overcome obstacles and conquer fears

Mama, you ain't gotta cry no mo', wipe them tears

I was once scared too, but now the coast is clear

All the ones who doubted me came and reappeared

And now they all screaming cheers, like we all drink beer

Like we ain't miss no time when we lost some years

And now they see me shine, wanna be standing here

And I'm just skipping the line, it's like I got clear

And I'm about to take off, I'm gettin' outta here

Y'all won't see me around

Ain't gon' see me be bound

People tryna ask questions seeing where I'm at now

But they won't ever know

As I keep laying low

I start to see everything that's out my control

And how love is the only way we should go

And how wisdom is the very thing we should hold

And how faith in God starts to generate hope

I can see how I'm loved now from all the love letters you wrote

NOTE TO SELF

What would your life look like if you only focused on the things that you thought were worth it?

REFLECTION

The day you came out of your mom's womb, God had a plan for you

He had to

It may have been hard for you to see it, being a little kid

And even more difficult to believe it when you look back at the things that you did

But it's true

I mean,

I can look at you and I can see you not the same

I can look at your lifestyle and I can see how much you've changed from who you
    used to be

Cause

Who you used to be

Is not who you are now

And that's why I'm so proud of you

Cause I've seen you

No . . .

I've watched you

I've watched you do things I know you're not proud of

Things that if Mom, Dad, Grandma, or Aunt ever knew about, they may just be
    ashamed of it coming from you

And I sat there

I sat there and watched you do it

And it wasn't until you gave your life over to God and tried to go hard for him for the
    first time that you began to realize exactly what you were doing

And as you began to cry about it after reading about it

I saw how it would eat you up on the inside not being able to talk about it to other
    people

And as you've gotten older, I've seen what it did to you

I seen how you put yourself in a box when it came to your relationship with God
    cause you ain't have nobody to teach it to you

So instead of it being a lifestyle that you live

You made it into a set of rules

Thinking there was things that you could and things that you couldn't do

And I don't know how, but somehow it ended up working out for you

Cause God just kept blessing you and blessing you and blessing you

Even when you had the wrong perspective about how living out this life really was,

Cause you was like them perfect ones

Tryna have the perfect relationship, the perfect conversation

Scared to be yourself cause you don't want to make a mistake and that's . . .

That's not right . . .

And I don't want you to feel like you gotta live in fear your whole life cause you
      don't want to make a mistake

I mean,

I can see it in your face you don't want to mess up anymore

And I can see how you held on to how you thought this Christian walk was
      supposed to look like for so long that now it's hard for you to let it go

Cause even when you try to live free, in the back of your mind it got you feeling like
      you're doing something wrong

But I'm the only one who sees that

It's hard for other people to notice that cause they're so focused on the impact that
      you have on people's lives

I mean,

You're leading people to Christ

You're inspiring them to want to have a better relationship with God

So whether you realize it or not

The things that you do are why you have so many people saying so many great
      things about you

Even if you don't believe some of the things they say about you

Cause the truth is you don't do some of the things they think you do

Like for one, you don't read like you should or pray like you could

And you don't go talk to people about Christ

And sometimes you feel like you're not even applying the word to your life

But what you *do* do is you live it out

And your lifestyle says more to people than the things you say out your mouth

Cause the truth is it's not about how you feel

Cause some days you gon' feel like you not living for him when the truth is you
really are

And you ain't gotta get caught up in people calling you a superstar

Just be who you are and stay true to yourself

Cause I don't know how far God is going to take you in life, but the higher that
he takes you, I don't want you feeling like you gotta go out there and be
somebody else

Cause being you

And doing what you do is why you got so many people looking up to you

And being you and doing what you do is . . .

It's another reason . . . uhh

Being you and doing what you do . . .

I just want you to know it's another reason why I look up to . . .

Bro, where'd you go?

Did you just walk out and leave, cause all I'm seeing right now is me

I turned for one second, and then I turned back around and now I'm starting to see
things differently

And this wasn't what I was seeing at the beginning, cause at the beginning I was
talking to you

Or maybe just maybe my vision was a little blurry

Cause ever since I've been honest, I'm starting to see things more clear

Which has me questioning: was I talking to you at all or was I talking to me all
along?

Cause I'm in front of this mirror
And I don't see you anymore
I see me
My reflection

NOTE TO SELF

It's okay to see yourself the way that you're seen by others.
Especially when it's about you having an impact on the lives of
people around you. You don't have to see yourself as a superstar,
but you can see yourself as an inspiration. Because that's what you
are to some people. And it's okay to accept that.

FAIR SHOT

Where I'm from, most people don't make it out

Some blame the system

I feel as if there is a system in place against us

Why is it designed for us to fail?

If that's the case, then why even dream?

Sometimes I wish my struggle wasn't with the system

Maybe then I would get a fair chance

But instead I was born in a game of life that I never chose

And now I must play the hand I was dealt

There's no kings in this game

We don't live with our fathers

And our mothers are worth far more than queens

The best card in my hand is the 2 of hearts

Which explains a mother's love for playing both roles

I've never seen a love like this

But that love won't teach me how to be a man

If I can be honest,

I get scared sometimes

I fear for my life more than being outside at night

There's drugs out there on the corners

Gang members on the streets

Sports is the only thing that keeps me safe

Meanwhile, some parents put their kids in sports just to have fun

But sports is my only way out

Without sports, there is no college

No degrees

No NFL

My life depends on a scholarship

We desire full rides more than women

What you may never understand is that . . .

This is my only chance

This is the best legal way that puts food on the table for a lifetime

If this doesn't work out,

I could be in jail for a lifetime

Not because I'm a bad person

It's just . . .

That's what the system does to people like me

Swallow me up only to spit me in jail

If we can be honest,

Without a degree

A corporation won't give people like me a chance

But drug dealers do

You think I want to sell drugs?

You think I want to get caught?

But how else am I going to provide for my family?

If it was up to me,

I'd rather be on a beach, though I've never seen a beach

But I bet you have

What else have you seen that I haven't?

Sometimes I just want to get away and see life in other states

But . . . unless it's through sports, I don't get to do that

But I bet you do

While you get to travel the world

I drive through my city

And while you have family dinners at home, I eat by myself

Now you see why I'm so closed off

Imagine wearing a hoodie not to be seen

But instead, people are scared of you

Tell me

How else am I supposed to hide my scars?

If I show my strength through tattoos, I'm seen as a thug

Which sounds like a lose/lose situation to me

But you

You're winning

And you haven't even done anything

So what makes you think that you're better than me?

I guarantee if we started from the same place,

I'd hold the key to your future

But since we don't, you hold the key to mine

Without the system you got it easy

But if we can be honest,

With the system against us

You not built like me

You not hungry like me

The only difference between me and you right now . . .

Is that you get a fair shot

And I don't

Remember that

NOTE TO SELF

Not everybody gets the same opportunity. Some are more blessed to start life in a better position than others. But never think that you're better than anyone. You'd be surprised what could happen if a person was given the same chance as you.

TURN OFF THE LIGHTS

Turn off the lights

Turn off the lights

He don't want y'all to see what's going on in his life

Turn off the lights

Turn off the lights

So I can see what living in the pitch black is really like

Cause my bro is in the dark and he been falling apart

Because the woman that he loves he let get too close to his heart

And now he don't know where to start

He got a lot on his mind

Like he told me that it's better if he'd be gone and that he commits suicide

Cause he been losing people left and right that brought him up in life

And he been tryna live for God, but he feels likes nothing been going right

So he feels like it's better he try to take his own life

He sending pictures to his wife of the pills he gon' take at night

Telling her to kiss his son Liam cause who knows if Daddy gon' ever see him again if
    he goes night night

Turn off the lights

Turn off the lights

He don't want y'all to see what's going on in his life

Turn off the lights

Turn off the lights

So I can see what living in the pitch black is really like

Cause my bro is in the dark and he been falling apart

Because the woman that he loves he let get too close to his heart

And now he feeling lost and he don't know what to do

And there's only three of us in the crew that he's really been talking to

And we've been tryna help him

But it's like he's so far gone

Taleeya said he overseas, he probably feelin' so alone

But I don't think he sees how killin' himself is wrong

But he said he tired of fighting and he just want to let it go

So he reaching out to us and we talking to him because we love him

But every time we try to help him, he be feeling like we judge him

And he telling us not to judge him

But just to walk with him

But if he jumps off that cliff,

We gon' have to jump off and get him

Turn off the lights

Turn off the lights

He don't want y'all to see what's going on in his life

Turn off the lights

Turn off the lights

So I can see what living in the pitch black is really like

Cause my bro is in the dark and he been falling apart

Because the woman that he loves want to let him go and start over

And now we're getting closer and closer to the edge explaining why he wants to off
himself so we can get it through our heads

Cause he wants us to accept it

Cause part of his life is hectic

He's over this God stuff, he said he losing his direction

And we don't know what to say back

We waiting on a text back

Cause he eight hours away and if we don't hear from him, we're afraid that he took
the pills

And if he did, then life about to get real

And I don't think he understands how a part of us feels

Cause if he take his own life, a part of us gon' be killed

And if he's gon' be gone forever, we gon' have to take care of his kids

So we need to

Turn on the lights

Turn on the lights

So he can see everything that's important in his life

Turn on the lights

Turn on the lights

So we can show him everything in the pitch black comes to the light

Cause my bro been in the dark and he been falling apart

But he been opening up and he been sharing his heart

And now it's time for us to start showing him the bigger picture

How his kids need him cause they need a father figure in their life right now

Cause when they grow up they wanna make their daddy proud

Like when they out there playing sports they want to see him in the crowd

And as long as he in the crowd, they got a smile on their face

And they'd rather struggle and have him around than to have Daddy far away

Cause they don't wanna look at pictures every day to see his face

And they don't want the only time they talk to Daddy to be when they pray

Turn on the lights

Turn on the lights

So we can show him everything that's important in his life

Turn on the lights

Turn on the lights

So we can show him everything in the pitch black comes to the light

Cause my bro been in the dark and he been falling apart

But he been opening up and he been sharing his heart

And I've been knowing this dude almost ever since the fifth grade

And it hurts so much how he says he wants to go away

Cause he told me this on Friday night

And I was textin' to him before I went out that night

And then I told my two bros the next day

And we was talking in the group the whole day

And all we could really say was just please don't do it, Bro, don't do it

You're not the only one in this world that's gon' have to go through it

Man, please don't do it

Bro, don't do it

You're not the only one in this world that's gon' have to go through it

But he said I'm in the dark

I'm falling apart

I gave her everything that I had and she took away my heart

And we said please don't do it

Bro, just don't do it

You're not the only one in this world that's gon' have to go through it

And he said y'all, I'm in the dark

And I'm falling apart

I gave her everything I had and she took everything I got

And now I'm feeling lost and I ain't got nowhere to go

I'm running for my life but I don't see no end zone

So we don't really know what the ending result is gonna be

I guess we gon' have to wait and see when he gets back from overseas

To be continued . . .

NOTE TO SELF

Not everything is going to be glitz and glamor. There's going to be heartache and pain. Even anxiety and depression. At some point, you're going to want to know if there's more to life than what you see and do every day. But what you have to do is find meaning in everything you do. You have to find a reason to live. If you focus only on the bad stuff in life, you are going to put yourself in a mind-set that results in not wanting to be here anymore. But you were created with a purpose. And that purpose was not to take your own life but to live a life of meaning.

WORKSHOP

1. Do you ever think about suicide? If so, why?

_____

_____

_____

_____

2. What makes you think life will be better for people without you?

_____

_____

_____

_____

3. If someone was going through the same thing you are right now, what would you tell them?

_____

_____

_____

_____

4. Have you reached out for help? Not just from friends but professional help?

_____

_____

_____

_____

WRITE DOWN REASONS FOR YOU
TO LIVE. AS MANY AS YOU CAN.
ONCE YOU DO THAT, FOR THE
NEXT THREE DAYS LIVE OUT AND
PURSUE THOSE "REASONS TO LIVE."
ALSO, FIND TWO PEOPLE
TO CONFIDE IN AND OPEN UP TO.
I WOULD SUGGEST A COUNSELOR
OR THERAPIST. JUST KNOW THAT
IN THIS LIFE YOU ARE NEVER ALONE
AND PEOPLE ARE HERE TO HELP.

LOSE YOURSELF

You ain't gotta be in a prison to know that you in a prison

Ignoring your intuition to follow a fake image of yourself that you created

Even though you just made it

Can you really say that you're being yourself?

I know that you got wealth and found a little help but you still care about people's opinions more than yourself

And that ain't really right, plus I know that you the type that likes to bottle up every emotion that you feel inside

So tell me what's really right

No, tell me what's really wrong

I know it's hard for you to let things go and just move on

So you keep on holding on to everything that you've known

But if you refuse to let it out, you just gon' explode

Just like a volcano

But why you gotta erupt?

It's people that's tryna help you, there's no need to fight and fuss

You ain't gotta sit and cuss, we just need to hash it out

If they take you for a joke, you just gotta laugh it out

I know life is scary now, that's why you keep passing out

GPS can't lead you to success, go find a different route

I know you tryna figure out what's the purpose in life

People go from broke to rich but still feel worthless in life

Situationships turn into emotional strife

Cheating is the only thing that men like

So now she's getting led on thinking one day she gon' be wifed

Suffering from a man that's her type

This about to be the fight of her life

Way bigger than a Mayweather fight

Where there are no draws

I know you hope sex is involved cause

All you wanna do is get in her drawers

This is a bigger picture than a painter can draw

Or what a therapist may think they can solve

This is life or death

Will you drown? Maybe not, but I ain't gon' hold my breath

I just know that things change when you stressed and depressed

All because you look for meaning in what you call success

While the things that made you in this life you hardly forget

Then you find yourself lost while you drunk and upset

Wondering where you go from here and what's gon' happen next

That's what life is like when you live with regrets

But everything can change if you live with respect

Loving one another as you can see how you're blessed

But until then, you gon' be stuck in this mess

If you keep fishing for things in life that you know you won't catch

NOTE TO SELF

What good is it to achieve so much in life if I can't even be myself? Why am I worried about living up to people's expectations? People lose themselves trying to please others. If I live to please others, then I'm never going to be free. And I'm tired of living in a prison.

1. Are you satisfied with your life?

_____

_____

_____

_____

2. Do you feel free? If not, what's holding you back from experiencing freedom in your life?

_____

_____

_____

_____

3. Do you talk about your problems? Or do you hold it in?

_____

_____

_____

_____

4. Why do you hold it in? Does it do you any good to hold it in?

_____

_____

_____

_____

BEFORE YOU GO TO BED AND WHEN YOU WAKE UP IN THE MORNING, TAKE 10 MINUTES TO CLOSE YOUR EYES AND IMAGINE YOURSELF BEING FREE. FREE FROM PROBLEMS, FREE FROM FEAR, FREE FROM WORRY, FREE FROM EXPECTATIONS, FREE TO LOVE, FREE TO BE HAPPY, FREE TO BE YOU.

IDENTITY CRISIS

Look

I can tell that you're lost and you're tryna find your way back

And as much as I want to be your man right now, I can't even say that

Cause I can tell that you're hurt

Your friends giving you lectures

But you can't even see your worth cause you ain't got your life together

I know

The feelings you got for me you can't show

Plus you at a place in life where you see how easy happiness can come and can go

And as you look for something real, trust I know just how it feels cause that's
    something that's hard for other people to show

That's why you gotta hold on to the things that you know

Cause that's the only thing in life that brings hope

But if you keep looking for something to fulfill you, they'll never see the real you and
    that's the road we like to take and go broke

But you don't have to quote me

You don't have to show me

I know your worth is far greater than any trophy

But you so messed up you got that mind-set like *show me*

And I can treat you like a queen if you really get to know me

I ain't worried about what's all in your jeans

I'm tryna show you things in life that you've never seen

So tell me, baby, are we a team?

She said look, you're a good guy, but nothing's ever as good as it seems

And it seems I can't compete with your past when every man you had then messed
    you up

I can't get a fair chance cause you think that I'm gon' stand you up

And I'm just tryna hold you down, how could I stand you up?

My cousin's saying *slow down* but I'm tryna show her God's got plans for her

Yeah, Tyler, but you might not be the man for her
Quit tryna force things before you get your heart tangled up
If she can't see her worth, then help her pick that angle up
Cause she gotta see what God sees before you can be that man for her

NOTE TO SELF

In this world, there will be heartache. However, don't put that heartache on other people who want to spend the rest of their life with you. They don't deserve the hurt and pain that came with your past relationship experiences. They deserve a fair chance.

WORKSHOP

1. Do you allow past relationships to affect how you treat people in new relationships?

_____

_____

_____

_____

_____

_____

2. If so, why?

_____

_____

_____

_____

_____

_____

3. Before a relationship, how do you see yourself?

_____

_____

_____

_____

_____

_____

4. After the relationship, how do you see yourself?

----

5. What changes?

----

6. What are you allowing in your relationships?

----

7. What's ruining your relationships?

FOR THE NEXT THREE DAYS, REFLECT ON YOUR PAST RELATIONSHIP EXPERIENCES AND SEE IF THERE IS A CYCLE. IF THERE IS A CYCLE, IDENTIFY IT. AFTER YOU IDENTIFY IT, ASK YOURSELF:

What needs to be changed?

_____

_____

_____

_____

_____

_____

How can I change it?

_____

_____

_____

_____

_____

_____

UNCOMMON

What's being gifted without a gift

Uber without a Lyft

Competitors come and go, but once you're purpose-driven, you should never lose
your grip

But hold on tight

And never lose your drive

Cause in this life they say only the strong survive

And if we gon' be in this together, let's see how far that we can thrive if we just
swallow our pride

No longer empty inside

I'm thinkin' who can tame us

These critics can't phase us

We got this grit that they can't teach, these people can't train us

We like this uncommon breed that they don't see

These people can't change us

All we hang around is stars, but they ain't all famous

So it don't matter who they wit', I rock wit' who I came wit'

Never been in this position, probably why I came quick

I like that yellow bone to go, you know that one that came thick

The one's my friends never got but wanna run a train wit'

But I ain't had sex, my wife gon' be the first I lay wit'

Though my friends would rather have a woman to play wit'

I say this like it's misleadin'

But people out here schemin'

They cut throats, no bleedin'

They up close wit' me dreamin'

They seein' that I'ma make it

She know my situation

We hang out, she think we datin'

I can't let these women play me

I started middle from the bottom

Won't let that become a problem

My family they know I got 'em

If money they need to borrow, ain't worried about no tomorrow

I'm gettin' betta each day

Tryna become elite, there's already too many greats

And if the critics gon' talk, then let them go ahead and throw shade

I got my city marching wit' me like we in a parade

And we gon' celebrate

And we gon' elevate

And we gon' keep the faith

Cuz no matter what them people throw our way

As long as we got God, we still gon' be straight

NOTE TO SELF

It's okay to be different. But it's not okay to fit in.

A NEW START

Are you tired of flowers and teddy bears?

Are you looking for a man that can show you that he cares through his prayers?

Knowing that the places that you want to go

He can take you there

Where no prenup or grocery store can ring up the love y'all share

To know just what you fighting for

How to get excited for

Something that no one else can have

I know that you been hurt in your past really bad

So before it could get worse, you been drawing red flags before emotions came

I just want to make sure that you ain't in no sunken place

From the things in life that happened to you in your younger days

Cause you so mature

I know now for sure

Every intention that I have in me is pure

Cause you shine like a diamond

And you the one I'm liking

Everything you have girl, I'm wifing

The way that we be vibin' got me thankful for the fall and thankful for the leaves as I
    stand here feeling like a tree

You get to see me naked . . .

And that's a deadly weapon

Truth is

I don't wanna hurt you

I know I got weeds to work through

Way more weeds than the people who smoke

When I say that I love you please don't take me for a joke

Cause I'm telling you that's what I know

That's what I feel

And I know what I'm feeling is real

You got way more to give than your sex appeal

And the way that you laugh and the things that you feel

Got me thankful for these voids I can't fill

You got me feeling elevated

You bring balance in me and hella patience

No more second-guessing, no more hesitating . . .

You shine just like the sun

In my life, you're defined as the one

I love you

NOTE TO SELF

Relationships aren't all about what you receive. It's also about what you give in return. If you aren't helping your future person grow, then you are holding them back from being their best self. If you really love them the way you say you do, then show them. Not by gifts, but by helping them reach their God-given potential.

SOMETHING IN THE MAKIN'

Please don't kill my vibe

All the pain and suffering that I'm dealing with inside I'm tryna hide

So please, can you just let it go?

I'm tryna go to a place that I ain't been befo'

The places where they beam and glow

And where stars shine

And as I lay there I wonder one day, *when will I shine?*

Is it true I can chase my dream, or am I wasting my time?

Should I go and make it happen or just wait for a sign?

A lot of people say they wait until they hear words from God

But there's times I feel like God just waits for us to decide

If we gon' live or just think it

Cause life's gotta be more than tryna dream it

But tell me what's after when we achieve it

Cause I refuse to live my whole life without meaning

So I'm making boss moves done in secret

I'm pregnant with success and I'ma keep it

And everything that stands in my way I'm gon' beat it like a drum

But there's some who don't think I'ma make it out of where I'm from

But little do they know that I'm as strong as they come

So let them keep talking

They do it so often

The only thing they care about in this life is just profit

But that won't get them nowhere without wisdom and knowledge

And as long as I got that in my life, then I'm solid

Cause I'ma stand firm in this faith I'm called in

If God gave his all for me, then I'm all in

No mo' talking

Foot on the gas, no breaks, ain't no mo' stopping

And no mo' parking

I'm tired of living life walking through all this darkness

Cause the world need a light

And we can't find the plug

So much hate in this world

We need more than a hug

We be looking for love in all the wrong places

Tryna fill these voids, but we got empty spaces

So we look for it in fame

We search for it in wealth

We look for it in things we can't find in ourself

And it's just so crazy all what I've seen lately

Got me wondering if we gon' ever make it

Cause some want thots

But I want basic

And for the gaps that can't be filled, I'll use braces

And I'll make sure that my life is straightened

And as I smile

I see myself, not just a child

But a masterpiece God created

Some gon' hate

But I'll embrace it

My time's coming

I been patiently waiting

Believe it or not

I'm gon' make it

But as of right now

I'm something in the making

NOTE TO SELF

There are no excuses. Either you want to live a purposeful life or you don't. Obstacles are a part of life. However, you have to learn which obstacles are meant for you and which ones are meant to be dodged. Don't waste your time fighting obstacles that were never meant to be fought. Focus your energy on what's important. What you focus on shows up the most in your life.

1. Are you waiting on God? Or is God waiting on you? Only you can answer that!

_____

_____

_____

_____

_____

_____

_____

_____

2. How far are you willing to go to reach your purpose in life?

_____

_____

_____

_____

_____

_____

_____

_____

GREEN PAPER

Note to self

How did I make it to the league

Then get caught up in this greed?

Chasing after everything

And even if it came to be, I'ma still be empty

And I'm wondering, is this why God sent me?

I grew up in a place where there was little

Where people only had a little

Four hundred dollars, that's a lot to them

Even though it's just a little

And rich folks comparing their money to other rich folks

That's pitiful

Never did I think I could see the struggle be so beautiful

And never did I think that I'd be in that situation

Back in high school I was just something in the making

Never thought that I'd be worried about the money that I'm making

Till they make you think happiness is found in the money that you making

Like, oh, you like your job?

Well how much are you making?

Oh, you don't like your job?

Nah, but you like the money that you making

Money is people's drive and also their motivation

But it's also the same reason for all the problems they be facin'

Cause it won't make you happy

And if you don't believe me

Go make however much money you can and watch people change in your family

And even friends

Friendships you thought would never end, all because you startin' to see this
money pilin' in

Green paper

Who knew that it could change a lot?

Green paper

It can make you buy a house, rent out a spot

Green paper

It's making girls change body parts

Green paper

It can change who you are

Green paper

It can make a girl drop it low

Green paper

Can really make a friend lose a bro

Green paper

Will have you spinning outta control

Green paper

That's what we choose over our Savior

Green paper, green paper, who knew that life would be like this?

Who knew that we would live like this?

But I'ma keep it one hundred, keep it trill like this

You the reason why people rob and steal like this

And why we kill like this

Play on these fields like this

Cause we want to see how it feels to live with this

So we can stunt with this

Buy blunts with this

For you we be on the corners selling drugs for this

Cause we lust for this

In the strip clubs for this

Women be tryna make these men bust for this

Cause we in love with this

Can't even trust with this

Many won't leave their spouse if they make too much of this

Green paper

Who knew that it could change a lot?

Green paper

It can make you buy a house, rent out a spot

Green paper

It's making girls change body parts

Green paper

It can change who you are

Green paper

It can make a girl drop it low

Green paper

Can really make a friend lose a bro

Green paper

Will have you spinning outta control

Green paper

That's what we choose over our Savior

NOTE TO SELF

Find purpose and the money will find you. Purpose gives you a reason to live and a reason to be happy. Finding money will only result in wanting more, because there will never be a price good enough.

THE MONSTER I CREATED

I created a monster. The type of monster that can defeat any doctor

No matter what type of pills they gave me, I still needed saving

I'm feeling bound, looking for something that can free myself

But the more I fear the monster, the more I can't even be myself

And as I look in the mirror, I can't even see myself

I just see a man who's lying to himself

Crying to himself

So many tears falling down his face, he can start his own ocean

And as I'm bound, panicky around,

Now the feeling is I'm hopeless

Broken

Like a toy that's never been opened

I'm waiting to be used, but don't know when I'ma be used

So now I sit, confused

Feeling mentally abused, tryna figure out

How I'm supposed to make it out

The key that sets me free is outta my reach

So I can't even break me out

I've always been a target, that's why Satan tryna take me out

But I'ma let this light shine, he ain't gon' put this flame out

Hiding gets you nowhere, that's the reason why I came out

And I won't let this monster get the best of me

I'ma fight this battle with what's left of me

I won't let anxiety become the death of me

Couple people thought that they was helping me, but all they did was lecture me

And one day I'ma talk about it, but for now don't pressure me

Dizzy and off balance in my head, that's how the pressure be

When I be overthinking things, that's why it be stressing me

But ever since that trauma came, it got me thinking less of me

That's why every time I go in public, I be getting panicky

But when I try to talk about it, they not understanding me

They just think I'm trippin'

That's why it's so depressin'

Cause if it ain't a text, they don't understand the message and

As I open up, I just be wanting them to see,

Everything that's been going on with me

Cause I'm so observant, but never in my life have I been perfect

And I understand the things we face in life will be worth it

But tell me, how do you fight when you just feel so defeated?

When anxiety's so strong you feel like you can't beat it

Cause your strengths that got you far in life have now become your weakness

And now my weaknesses I gotta tend to

You may understand the things I've been through

But it's hard to help me if you don't understand that mental side

When you feel less alive

Cause it seems like you're dying inside

Cause your heartbeat's racing

And your body keeps shaking

And now you feeling like it's a hundred degrees

And your doctor's saying taking a Xanax is the only thing that you need

But if we can be honest, that isn't gon' solve anything

Cause the monster I created can withstand anything

All because it's fueled by all of my fears

And now I gotta fight just to keep my mind clear

Otherwise I'ma have to deal with ringing all in my ears

And though it looks like I'm doing good, it ain't what it appears

I been dealing with this just past a year

And now I gotta fight for my life if I wanna be free

Cause this monster that I'm facing is the other side of me

And the only way that I can beat it

Is if I rely on my weakness

This is the fight of my life

NOTE TO SELF

If you created the monster, you can destroy the monster.

WORKSHOP

Ways to control anxiety:

1. Meditate.

2. Focus on your breathing.

3. Meditate by focusing on an object for however long you choose.

4. Live in the moment.

5. Instead of running from what you're afraid of, just face it.

6. Take a step back from the problem and breathe, which will allow you to create space.

7. Just live and try not to worry about it.

8. Find the triggers that set your anxiety off.

UNCONTROLLED ANXIETY IS SOMETHING THAT WE CREATE, AND IF WE CREATE IT, THEN WE CAN CONTROL IT. CHALLENGE IT. FOCUS ON WHAT'S HAPPENING RIGHT NOW INSTEAD OF CREATING IN YOUR HEAD WHAT MIGHT HAPPEN. SOMETIMES WE DO THAT, AND WHAT WE THOUGHT WAS GOING TO HAPPEN DOESN'T EVEN HAPPEN. SO DON'T WASTE YOUR ENERGY STRESSING ABOUT THINGS THAT HAVEN'T EVEN HAPPENED.

TOGETHER WE RISE

If we rise, then who falls?

And who answers the phone if we call?

Look, I know people might tell y'all their side of the story

But who knows what they really saw?

Cause what I saw could be a deal-breaker

And now I gotta get my thoughts together

But if you wanna know, then I'll try to tell ya

How my destiny and dreams both got togetha

Cause when I met my dreams I found my destiny

And she allowed me to see the best of me

Then I met my purpose and he fell in line

Cause he liked how my destiny and dreams stayed next to me

And now I'm at the place where I wanna be

And I know exactly who I'm gonna be

And who I'm gonna reach

And who I'm gonna teach

Now y'all lookin' at me like, boy, you better preach

But if I preach it, then I gotta live it

Because a lot of people gon' pay attention

But if I live it right, then they'll realize that Jesus Christ is the one they're missin'

And if he the missing piece, then they can finish that puzzle

And dudes ain't gotta go on them streets to hustle

And lift product while they pushing weight

Then flexing on 'em showing us their muscles

Cause eventually they gon' get in trouble

But if you want to help them, first you got to understand their struggle

Before you call a play and then touchdown

You gotta first learn how to run the huddle

Because some people not gon' play with you

If they feel like they can't even relate with you

But if they hang wit' you, then you're reliable

And sometimes you might have to call an audible

Cause life don't always happen the way you expect it to

Like look to your left that's a prostitute

And she let dudes hit it for a prize or two

But she say she gotta do what she gotta do

So you tell me

Everybody wanna know what you see

Do you see her for the woman that she is right now?

Or do you see her for the woman that she could be?

Cause two words could change everything

"I do" plus a wedding ring

And one ring is worth more than one night

And the vows she speaks is worth more than any price

And now she could see what her life is like

She got a good husband

Got a good life

Got a good job

She got kids at home

Now she realizin' she a good wife

And the man who found him a wife found him a good thing

And they could both tuck their kids in to sleep at night, man, that's a good thing

But I know a kid who would give anything just to experience that same thing

But he was brought up in a single-parent household and now he want to know *is that a black thing?*

And if it's a black thing, do you think that'll ever change?

And if not, can you help the people understand what it's like for a kid to talk on the phone with his dad as much as he can?

Cause Daddy can't tuck him in to sleep at night like the other family

So Mama gotta do the best she can and teach him how to be a man

And Mama tryna teach him before the streets teach him

Cause if the streets reach him, life gon' get real for him

Cause he gon' be around shooters who gon' kill for him

And what's the point of tryna sit here and feel for him?

If you gon' feel for him, then do something about it

Before he goes out in this world and commits all of this violence

But if you decide not to help him

You might as well have been the one to pull the trigger and kill him if you're gon'
remain quiet

Cause if you remain quiet, BANG

You hear the sirens

There go another family cryin'

Maybe it would have been different, Tyler, if you didn't stay quiet

Cause if you didn't stay quiet

You could stop some of these riots if you just get up on stage and talk about this
violence

And so I just decided to finally talk about it

Cause if I talk about it, then I gotta *be* about it

But before I can make a difference in this world

I gotta realize that one life matters

And if one life matters, then I found a solution

And we can all come together as one and we can start a revolution

Saying no more lies

No more envy

No more hatred

No more enemies

No more jealousy

No more felonies

No more killings

No more prisons

No more suicide

No more death penalty

No more probation

No more molestation

No more rapin'

No more baby mamas

No more baby daddies

No more kids havin' to be brought up in single families

No more domestic violence

No more riots

No more guns

No more wars

We can't fight with hate

We gotta fight with love

We can win wit' love

We can bring back peace

We can work together to get people off of these streets

We could bring back hope to a dyin' breed

Togetha we can rise up and change everything

Cause I ain't worried no mo' about this American Dream

It's time to take back what's God's and bring back his dream

So let's rise up

NOTE TO SELF

You can't always wait for somebody to help fight for what you believe in. You have to be willing to take the first steps. You might look crazy at first. But everyone looks crazy in the eyes of others until they achieve what they set out to achieve.

THE WRONG TYPE OF LOVE

Nobody said that this life would be easy

I can tell you going through it but know I'm here if you need me

You got a good heart, I can tell by how you treat me

At times I think you like me, though your actions mislead me

I know you used to get hit on and it would go on for some years now

So when it comes to any man, you be living all in fear now

Scared to be tough

Don't want it to result in another beatdown

Scared to speak up so you store it all deep down

Hard to close your eyes when that's the only thing you see now

Crying in the bed, that's the way you fall asleep now

Can't even go to church cause you don't wanna see a man

Plus, when the preacher say "amen"

It got you thinking 'bout a man

And I can't understand this feeling that you feel

A love that was once so deep and something real turned to a horror film

And now it's hard for you to let it go

As much as you want to talk about it, you don't want everyone to know

But

Nobody said that speaking up would be easy

I know you wish it never happened, but in life there's no genies

You got a good heart, I can tell by how you treat me

If you ever wanna talk, just know I'm here if you need me

Cause I see the scars

And I see the marks

And there's no way that this man should have the key to your heart

I know you ain't seen this side when you was with him from the start

But ever since he put his hands on you

You been falling apart

And I watched how you would hide

I've seen how you cried

And how you start to tense up soon as he walks by

And he say that he gon' change

But you know that's a lie

And you feel the only way out is staying right by his side

But I wanna let you know that there's another way

That you ain't gotta feel bound and think that you a slave

There's people in this world that know the things you face

And they're here to help you

And let you know that you are brave

Cause you are very strong

And you're never alone

I know you feel it was a mistake when at first it was a happy home

With the feeling he'd always be there for you to lean on

And even though you're scared, you ain't gotta be afraid no mo'

We gon' be by your side before and after you let him go

NOTE TO SELF

There are people in this world who want to know that people care about them. Be that person for someone. Help them. Go the extra mile with them. Be that person to them that you want others to be for you. And if you see something that's not right, speak up!!

I'M COMING HOME

Hear our voices

Here's our choices

If they talkin' jibber-jabber, just block out their noises

I've seen bloodshed, you know, the color of roses

A staff at these people's hands, but they don't look like Moses

They don't want to make a way and clear that path that chose us

They just want us to stay so this new pharaoh can hold us

I really be feeling like these people tryna control us

Cause when we speak our minds, that's when they start to oppose us

But Jesus upholds us

We on a rollercoaster

This world's tryna hold me down, but see I'm 'bout to divorce her

I'm tryna get myself up, but girl, I ain't gonna force ya

No more ash on my skin, cause I got that moisture

Yeah, I got that lotion

But that girl needs hope and

She readin' Jesus daily cause she needs a devotion

But see me, I'm devoted

Well, I'm getting devoted

I'm living for God again, but I just gotta stay focused

Can't worry about tomorrow, gotta live in the moment

Gotta gift I've been working on and it's time to show it

Cause I've been on it

And I know they want it

No more window-shopping, today's the day we own it

But never forget how back in the day we would try it

Before we would buy it

Cause momma wasn't wasting money if we didn't like it

But now that I got bread, I know it feels excitin'

Who would've ever thought a Lexus be the car I'm drivin'?

And even though I'm livin' good, don't mean I gotta fly private

As long as I'm with God, I'm gon' make it in his timing

So let the haters hate and let the greats just stay silent

The dates on their calendar could never tell the end, just ask the Mayans

The worst murder untold was somebody who stayed quiet

Who could've brought change but decided to stay silent

But Dr. King spoke love against all of this violence

But Jesus, come back, take us home, be our pilot

There's too many people dyin'

Too many families cryin'

And they looking to the sky and just askin' you *why?*

And they don't understand how you can still have a plan

But you're the one who brought hope and who causes us to stand

So I thank you in advance for even givin' us a chance

To learn everythin' about you in this world we livin' in

Cause this life is full of sin

And we dyin' in our sins

But you died for our sins

So I'm dyin' to this sin

So my new life can begin

Lord, I won't change

I'm tired of all this change

I'm learnin' money can't bring us happiness in these later days

And that's somethin' I should've known, but I had to get it inside my brain

So Lord, I'm comin' home

I just hope that it ain't too late

NOTE TO SELF

No matter what you do in life, people are always going to have something to say. If you pursue your dream, people are going to talk. If you don't pursue your dream, people are going to talk. So just know that no matter what, the critics will never stay silent.

RELATIONSHIP GOALS

Truth is I'm just a regular dude

Real laid-back and cool

No disrespect to Lauren London

But I don't be on that new new

Except I'm talking about them shoes and the chains they buy

And the Range they drive

With their girl on their side

And people showing off their pride cause they really want that ride

But what we don't realize is we don't get to see their real lives

All we see is their women

And the women might be lookin' at him different cause he made it

So we don't even get to see her real eyes

Cause she focused on the prize

Plus, her motives are in disguise

But we just watching from the side hoping that one day we can drive ourselves

Cause we want to be able to model ourselves after them

And finally be able to get a model ourselves

Cause she postin' pictures on the 'gram tryna model herself

And I'm diving in her DMs and I ain't talkin' Michael Phelps

But I'm going for the gold

She just responded back, she said she a woman that got goals

So I hope that we can kick it

Cause if we get to kick it, I feel like I scored a goal except I ain't playin' soccer

Uh-oh

She hit me back again and told me that she got a daughter

And she livin' for God now, she left her past up at the altar

So if she let me in her life, she making sure I won't stop her

Or be like them crazy people in her life that be tryna pop up

But I told her if I fall for her, then don't expect me to pop up fast

Especially if I think it's gon' last

And she said well, if it does, then I want you to meet my dad

And I'm thinkin' to myself, she could be the best I ever had

But at the same time, I hope she don't want me for this cash

Cause if that's the case, I'd rather her just not write me back

Cause I don't want to put myself in a position to deal with that

And go around in circles kinda like we runnin' track

Cause I'm in my own lane

And this is my habitat

But she told me she been struggling and having habits that might break her

But I told her not to let them habits break her

And if she needs a superhero, I know someone who can save her

Cause we got a savior who saved us

Who created us from the dust

That's how he made us

So baby, let me take you to lunch

I know where to take us

We can order the food after they get us fruit punch

Baby, this is love not lust

Let's make it marvelous

Look, I don't want us to fall in lust

But if we fall in lust,

Then sin leveled us

But we can level up

And if we leveled up,

Then we pedaled up to the top of the hill

Where old scars and old bruises can be given time to heal

And you ain't got to open up cause I know just how you feel

You the woman I want to spend the rest of my life with

And that's real

And we can open up together so that people can see the real

And they can watch our lives like a highlight reel

So that way they can learn everything that they need to know

Cause as long as God got us at the top

They gon' be looking up to us for relationship goals

NOTE TO SELF

Don't get caught up in what other people do. How they live is how they live. How you live is how you live. You don't have to be like them. You don't have to be flashy. People don't have to know that you got money. At the end of the day, just be you. Live how you want to live.

WORKSHOP

1. What does a successful relationship look like to you?

_____

_____

_____

_____

2. Is it better to have a private relationship or a public relationship?

_____

_____

_____

_____

3. Is helping each other a part of your relationship?

_____

_____

_____

_____

4. Are you dating with a purpose? Or dating just to date?

_____

_____

_____

_____

WEAK SPOTS

I told you I had a girl

But you still didn't care

At first you acted like you did

Then you tried to take advantage of me

Is it cause you seen how happy I was?

Why is it because your life is messed up

You want to mess up mine?

Is it cause you want me to feel miserable like you?

Believe it or not,

I'm better than that

You may never see that

And that's okay

I just wish that you could look at yourself and see what I see

Cause you look lost

You have no identity

No direction in life

It's like you're miserable, without a purpose

What you fail to realize is that sex is not an achievement

But you treat it like an NBA season

Except there is no trophy at the end

Just heartache

And pain

You try to fill a void only to make it bigger

Without knowing that sex is undefeated

It's not a game that you should play with

You may think you're in control right now

But you're not

Except you use it to cope with your problems

All that shows me is that you have no morals

Is that how you were brought up?

Pleasing every single guy that has money until one makes you a wife?

Life's gotta be more than looking for a come up

But you can't hear that from me

Cause once you did what you did,

You missed out on a good friend

However, you probably won't notice that until you hit rock bottom

I just hope one day someone comes into your life to help you see what God sees

Cause that's what you need right now . . .

Not sex

NOTE TO SELF

People will take advantage of you if they know your weak spots.

Ask yourself the following questions and make a list for each.

1. Do you know your weak spots?

----

2. Do people ever take advantage of your weak spots?

----

3. How can you avoid being taken advantage of?

DIFFERENT MEANINGS

One's innocence

Is another man's opportunity

One's assumption

Is believed more than the truth

One's mistake

Is another man's strength

One's attentive ear

Is another man's judgment

One's guilt is not based on regret

But stems from the fact they got caught

One's lie is received as "I believe you"

To the other, the lie says "I love you"

One's trust is based on rules

That's how insecurities are not seen

One's word can be meaningful

But to another misleading

"I got you" means "I'm not leaving your side."

To others, it's used for confirmation

A person's "Why?" can be seen as "Why me?"

To others, it's referred to as their motivation

"No" means "no"

But to some, it's seen as curiosity

"Stop" means "stop"

But how you say it can be seen as a turn-on

Rejection makes you feel worthless

To others, it saves them from heartache

One living with both parents is normal

To another, it's very surprising

Marriage is seen as love

To others it's a business decision

One views a prenup as a way of escape

But to another, it's the only way they can trust them

What one considers ugly,

Another considers beautiful

What one sees as too much,

Another sees as enough

What you refuse,

Another accepts

Sports is a way of exercising,

But to another it's their life

Profanity is taken to heart,

But to others it's just the way they speak

One's job can be seen as another man's way out

For instance,

Drug dealing is a crime

But to some, it's their only way to put food on the table

What one considers to be dirty,

Another sees as clean

When one wants more it's so they're not complacent

But to another, it symbolizes greed

One sees himself as poor when compared to others

But another sees himself as rich

What you see

May not be what others see

And that's okay!

NOTE TO SELF

Words have different meanings to different people. How you view something isn't how somebody else views it. And that's okay. It doesn't mean that it's wrong.

LIFESTYLE

I see the glitzes and the glamors

I see the money, power, and fame that come with this lifestyle,

Look at all the people holding their cameras

Some of 'em glad that we made it

Other people can't stand us

They judge us based off of what they see but they don't know a thing about us so
   how can they really understand us?

See we talk this talk that they may never speak

And we've seen so many things they'll probably never see

And we got this type of blood that they may never bleed

And these aims that we got in life they may never reach

So how can you see what it's like to be me if you ain't never been in my position?

When it's easier to put myself in a box and try to live

Than to go out here in this world and try to be free

See I'd rather just keep myself in a prison

Cause there's too many people who know me and they're watching me

And I don't talk much on social media, but they followin' me

So what am I supposed to do?

These people are intrigued by the things that I do

They tryna keep up with my life

They tryna watch my every move

So now I got to be careful in the things that I share

And who I hang around and who I conversate to

Cause nowadays people will go outta their way just to find a story to write about you,

So now I got to figure out the ones that's really for me

I mean, I know I got God, my family, and some of the people I call my homies

But I gotta watch out for them people who talk to me just to go and tell other
   people that they know me

And it's crazy that these women I used to want back in the day growing up didn't
    necessarily want me, but now that I made it, they hitting me up and they telling
    me that they want me
But I'd rather just focus on a girl that don't already know me
But chances are, who am I gonna find in this world that don't already know me?
Cause the way that we be texting, I could tell that they want me, I just don't know if
    they want me for me or if they want me for the money
Cause this lifestyle can make anybody interested
Cause they see how you live, and now they want to live like this
So when you invite 'em to the house and it seems like y'all about to have sex, don't be
    surprised when she don't ask you where yo condoms at
Cause it's like she wants you to get her pregnant
She wants to have your kid
And you ain't got to believe me, but some of these girls will stoop that low
Not because they like you, but because they want to trap you so they could get you
    for that child support
But I know not every girl is like that
You got some girls that are independent, but the thing is I hung out with a girl who
    said she was like that
She told me she wanted her life to be private, so I took her phone to
    show her how my life wasn't private, and I saw she looked up my NFL contract
So let me just take a step back for a minute and reevaluate my life and get away
    from all these women
Cause Lord knows, it's hard to figure out any of their intentions
Cause some of 'em hit me up and they fail to mention that they already messed
    with my bros before, and if that's the case, then I can't even take you serious
If you don't want me for me, then you hitting me up for the wrong reasons
And as athletes we already got this stereotype that most of y'all already believe in
But y'all don't really know what it's like to be in this position

All y'all really seeing is the life that we be living on Instagram and Twitter

Some of the athletes having a little fun with the models and the strippers

And that's the life that we be living

And that's the life that y'all be wanting

So you looking for an athlete, you know the ones that be stunting

The ones who be throwing all this money, buying all these cars

Up in VIP livin' it up with all these broads

And now you finally in and you finally get to feel a part of all the glitzes and glamours

You around people that got a little bit of money, power, and fame, and you want everybody to see it so you record them with your cameras

Some of y'all feel like y'all made it only cuz y'all around us

While everybody else looking in judges us based off of what they see, but they don't know a thing about us, so how can they understand us?

See, we talk this talk that they may never speak

And we done seen so many things they'll probably never see

And we got this type of blood that they may never bleed

And these aims that we got in life they may never reach

So how can you see what it's like to be me

If you ain't never put on my shoes?

You sit there and talk about how athletes go broke

But do you really know what it's like to be used when people asking you for money cause they know that you got it?

My bro just said he needs help to get his feet back up and he's wondering if I could spot him

And he said he'll pay me back

But I told him, naw, Bro, you don't need to

Only to find out he asked everybody in our crew and now I'm looking at myself like dang, Lock, he just schemed you

Got this crazy look on my face like, man, why you gotta do me like that?

I thought me and you was brothers, you ain't have to use me like that

But the older that you get, the more you start to learn that things change once you
get that NFL contract

Cause they don't look at you the same

Nah

They don't see you as the same kid that they grew up with way back in the day

You made all this money, now they're looking at you like you from a different place

But you got some kids that's looking up to you cause they see how you paved the way

And they tryna make it out just like you and do the same

But other people looking at you cause they hope that you can make a way

Cause they need a little help and they looking at you like you the bank

Cause you got that type of money that you can do for them what a lot of people can't

And they looking at it like, what is it to you if you pay for some of my bills?

What is it to you if you pay for some of my meals?

But they don't understand that when you lend a helping hand, people try to take
advantage of you and they don't understand how it feels

Cause when you look at it from our perspective

They just asking us for money cause they know that we got it

But they don't understand that more money causes more problems

And I see that people need help to pay the rent,

But they can't always be expecting me to drop them dollars

Cause doing that ain't well spent for me

Cause I'm out here tryna chase a dream and I got people tryna let 'em get
beside me and all, but I ain't tryna let 'em get in between

Cause I gotta get it by any means and by any means I mean necessary

So some of y'all got to be secondary

Cause I'm focused right now on the primary, and the primary can be very scary, but
everything I need I got in my genes, so I guess you could say it's hereditary,

Cuz I'm out here tryna be legendary . . .

I said I'm out here tryna be legendary so I can step up, maybe talk now

Everybody think I'm in the zone now

I'm just out here tryna make my mama proud

And I'm still tryna make my mama proud

And I ain't even been home in a while now but I ain't scared to say it

I need to go help these kids at home

All the ones like me that's tryna make it cause who knows, maybe I could be
their inspiration

I was born in Tulsa, I made it out, I can give advice, maybe help 'em out

I remember when I was living up in Mimi's house and my mom and pawpaw was
up in Mimi's house and I was out there tryna take a different route

I wasn't tryna get caught in that peer pressure

I wasn't tryna smoke, I wasn't tryna drink, I was tryna get my dreams together,
cause there wasn't too many people who believed in me

Who believed in me?

I only had my friends and my family

It was too many people who was caught in this legacy

That my dad and uncle had already set for me

So people didn't know what to expect for me

Until I gave my life to God and then they realized that he had everything already set
for me

So I'm walking now in my purpose and I'm thankful for everything I got because

I realized now it's a blessing, and when much is given, much more is required, but
now people coming at you for the wrong reasons

And I ain't tryna get caught in that girl's smile, I don't wanna get lost in that lifestyle

Cause I see the glitzes, I see the glamors

I see the phones, I see the cameras, I see why they don't understand us

Because they ain't never seen life in this perspective

But when you make money, things change
People need help, and they ask away
And if you say no, then they'll say you changed
Mostly cause they don't look at you the same
Cause when you make money, things change
People need help and they ask away
Mostly cause they want to see a better day
And if you say "no," then they'll say you changed
Welcome to the lifestyle

NOTE TO SELF

Some people will never understand what it's like to be in this lifestyle. Where there's opportunity in one area, there's loss in another. What are you willing to gain, and what are you willing to lose?

NO MORE HIDING

Truth is I'm just like you

I'm just another flawed human

Who likes to make mistakes and live with regrets then look in the mirror, like *what am I doing?*

I've got thoughts that run wild more than my imagination

Fears that follow me more than my shadow

And as I begin to fight myself within

I'm realizing I'm not prepared for this battle

And though I could run, it'd be harder to find

Freedom in life with a peace of mind

So I stay true, climb one or two

Mountains just to get me a new view

To buy a new house and get a new car

Light the world up and shine like a star

Most people thought that I wouldn't go far

Most people thought I'd be in my backyard

But I go to the bank, get a withdrawal

Never say "can't," forget what they thought

You got the money and that's what you bought

You go and cheat and hope you don't get caught

But my girl gotta body, I like her mind

Girls like that, they harder to find

And she got faith so we gon' be straight

But do I still give her a prenup to sign?

Maybe I do, maybe I don't

But tell me what happens if she tells me "no"?

Should I still do it? Or not pursue it?

I just don't want a marriage to be ruined

If I can lose half,

She can get half

And right now she's the best thing that I have

And I don't wanna split

Ball's in my court and I don't wanna brick and I don't wanna miss

Cause I don't want a chick that I gotta go fish

And I gotta admit

Bills get paid and the money gets spent, but it don't go to rent

And I got some friends in my pockets

And that stuff happens too often

They know how much money I be making

And if you ask me, they be talking

But they saying that I'm their last option

And this their last time and they stopping

Then two or three months go by

And they all back in my pockets

And I'm tired of going through my wallet

And I'm tired of being their bank

Even though they say that they gon' pay me back

I already know that they can't

But at some point this gotta end

Cause I'm tired of getting my dawg outta the pen

And if I find out they keep using me

They gon' lose out on a real friend

NOTE TO SELF

You can lie to people, but you can't lie to yourself. Being honest with yourself is the way to living free.

FLY HIGH

Spoken word

You can have your own flow

And you ain't got to be rich just to be happy

You can still be broke

If you're lost but still alive, then you can still find hope

But don't live to survive

You got to learn how to fly

You got to spread your wings

Go out there and chase your dreams

The higher that you fly, a new perspective you gon' see

And the perspective that you see

It's right there for you to reach

But don't get caught up in those people who can't see the same thing

Just fly high

Just fly high

Cause when you small like a kid, everything looks big

But when you go up to the sky, you see everything for what it is

So fly high

No matter what, just fly high

And make sure that you always got a dream

Always got a plan

Always got a vision though people may never understand until they see just how
    you livin'

Now look at you in this position

And all them people who doubted you saying they was the ones trippin'

Cause you always stood tall

Always had faith

Never listened to their opinions but you learned from their mistakes

And you knew what was at stake

You've been fighting your whole life

Showing the world God is real by the way you live your life

And you understand the price that was made for you

How Jesus died on the cross and your sins was paid for you

So go out there so we can see everything that's made in you

Cause everybody waiting to see the great in you when you fly high

When you fly high

Cause when you small like a kid, everything looks big

But when you go up to the sky, you see everything for what it is

So fly high

No matter what, just fly high

And make sure that you never give up

But you always stay strong

And that you always put in the work

But that's something that you've been doing all along

Tryna be by people's side even when they do you wrong

And though it hurts your heart, you're still tryna hold on to the very thing that got
   you here

But that don't mean you should live in fear

Injuries come and go, but one day, Lock, they gon' disappear

But that don't mean you sit there and compare yourself to the way that everybody
   else live

Or the money that they got

And how they got to buy a big crib

Just be you

And do the things that you do

Don't worry about other people's gifts

Just stay true to you and fly high

Just fly high

Cause when you small like a kid, everything looks big
But when you go up to the sky, you see everything for what it is
So fly high
No matter what, just fly high

NOTE TO SELF

Life is all about perspective. Perspective is reality. If you want to change your perspective, you've got to change what you see.

1. What does flying high mean to you?

_____

_____

_____

_____

_____

2. Are you flying high? Or are you flying at a comfortable height?

_____

_____

_____

_____

_____

3. What would your life look like if you flew high?

_____

_____

_____

_____

_____

IT'S TIME TO GET OUT OF YOUR COMFORT ZONE. THE HIGHER YOU FLY, THE MORE YOU SEE. FOR THREE DAYS, FIND SOMETHING TO FOCUS ON THAT GETS YOU OUT OF YOUR COMFORT ZONE.

BEAM AND GLOW

Shawty so cold with it

I introduced myself and ran game, but she said she's too old for this

I said, yeah, but I ain't the same

She said, where you tryna go with this?

I said, I'm tryna be your main

She said, I can tell you ain't a pro at this

I said, yeah, but I ain't tryna play no games

She said, but you don't even know me yet

I said, that gives me time to pick your brain

She said, but I don't even owe you that

I said, f'sho

Well I just want you to know

That I ain't seen no one like you befo'

You the type of woman that don't need makeup just to beam and glow

You got that natural look

That angle-to-capture look

I'm reading how you transformed like I'm in an action book

I'm diggin your style

And no, I'm not in no fashion book

But I see when you smile

That I'm feeling your actual look

You got that mind that I ain't never seen

And it's your heart that makes you a queen

And I just want you to know . . .

That's what makes you beam and glow

And even though you barely know me

Girl, I see you as a trophy

But not something to play for

Not something to win

You the type that keeps a man faithful to the end

Though you had some bad relations and dealt with some temptations

Having a woman like you is what keeps a man being patient

Cause a man that finds a wife finds him a good thing

And girl, you're more important than what a ring can ever bring

And if I get the chance to know you, then I can finally show you

How beautiful the new you is and the old you

So do you like to talk? Or are you not social?

If you like old school, we can dance like old folks do

And if you can't relate

I'll teach you how to skate

But it all depends on if you say "yes" to this date

I can treat you like a queen, baby, give me a chance

I'm not like them other men tryna get in your pants

But what I'm not gon' do is sit here and pressure you

I'm not gon' lecture you

You should know I mean business just by how I stepped to you

I just need a chance

She said, yeah but what's that gon' do?

I said everything you need to see is legible

I ain't 'bout to show you what my debit or credit do

That's the stuff that other men that want you try to do

I ain't gon' lie to you

I ain't gon' hide from you

I ain't 'bout to waste my time and show you what I can do

Though you got trust issues, you keep asking what I can do

I'ma lead you to God so you see what's inside of you

So you can beam and glow

NOTE TO SELF

If you want something, then go pursue it. Don't let fear stop you from possibly spending the rest of your life happy. Sometimes you can get scared of rejection. But who says rejection always has to be a bad thing? You should be happy when a person says "no"! Why? Because God protected you from something that wasn't meant for you! You don't have to change who you are or even try to be someone else. At the end of the day, the only thing that I want you to know, Tyler, is that you are good enough. And, eventually, someone will see that and marry you. But until then, God sees that. Now it's time for you to see it.

1. Write down all the things that you like about yourself.

_____

_____

_____

_____

_____

_____

_____

_____

_____

_____

2. Write down all the things that you don't like about yourself.

_____

_____

_____

_____

_____

_____

_____

_____

_____

_____

LAST ASSIGNMENT

Look at all the things you don't like about yourself as you turn the last page in the book.

As you look at all the things you don't like about yourself, I want to encourage you to love the things about you that you dislike. God sees you as a masterpiece, and it's time for you to see yourself the way he sees you!!

The only thing you have to change is how you see yourself!

ACKNOWLEDGMENTS

God, I truly want to say thank you for everything. I couldn't have ever imagined my life being the way it is now. As I've gotten older, I've realized that bad things aren't really bad at all. They're only bad if we see it that way. Life is about perspective. I've learned that the greatest perspective we can ever have in this world is seeing everything the way you see it. There's power in how you see things. There's confidence in how you see things. I can see myself for who you created me to be. And also see hope in each and every person.

God, I thank you for the family that you have blessed me with. I wouldn't trade them for the world. They are truly the best support system that I could ever have. They made everything look easy. From raising me as a kid to making it to the NFL, their support has never wavered. They are truly something special. I wish my family members who passed away could experience everything that's happening in my life. But I know that you're in heaven cheering for me every step of the way. To all my family, I want to say from the bottom of my heart, "I LOVE YOU ALL."

God, I want to say thank you for the friends that you've placed in my life. They are truly something special. They make the struggle look beautiful. They know how to have fun with NOTHING. Which makes having fun with MORE easy. That's one of the best things we could've learned growing up. To all my friends, thank you for being just who you are. I LOVE YOU ALL.

God, I see now how you have a plan for each and every person. I can also see now that everything does work for the good for those who love you and are called according to your purpose (Romans 8:28). Thank you for allowing me to experience all of these things in life. Thank you for allowing me to serve you! You are truly everything to me. And I want to say THANK YOU!!!! With everything in me I want to say, "I LOVE YOU."

— Reflections of Tyler Lockett

ABOUT THE AUTHOR

Tyler Lockett is an NFL All-Pro wide receiver and return specialist for the Seattle Seahawks. Originally from Tulsa, Oklahoma, Lockett played football at Kansas State University, where he set school records for career receiving yards, career receptions, and career receiving touchdowns. Off the field, Lockett has hosted free youth football camps and is an ambassador for a variety of charitable causes, receiving multiple nominations for the Art Rooney Sportsmanship Award. Lockett has been performing poetry since his teenage years, and he appears at open mics and poetry slams in the Seattle area. He hopes that his poetry expresses his love of God, and brings hope and inspiration to readers of all ages and backgrounds. *Reflection* is his first book.

Andrews McMeel Publishing
a division of Andrews McMeel Universal
1130 Walnut Street, Kansas City, Missouri 64106

www.andrewsmcmeel.com

19 20 21 22 23 BVG 10 9 8 7 6 5 4 3 2

ISBN: 978-1-5248-5406-5

Library of Congress Control Number: 2019941721

Editor: Lucas Wetzel
Art Director: Holly Swayne
Production Editor: Julie Railsback
Production Manager: Cliff Koehler

ATTENTION: SCHOOLS AND BUSINESSES
Andrews McMeel books are available at quantity discounts with
bulk purchase for educational, business, or sales promotional use. For information,
please e-mail the Andrews McMeel Publishing Special Sales Department:
specialsales@amuniversal.com.